The
NORTH YORKSHIRE
MOORS RAILWAY
Past and Present

Map of the NYMR and associated lines

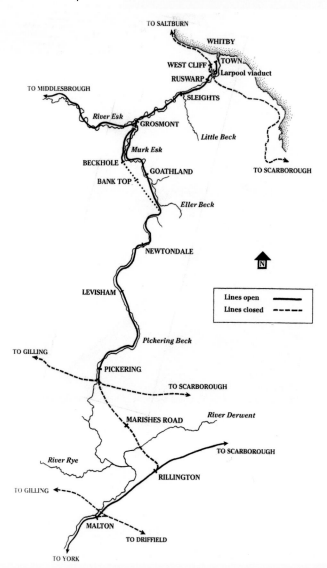

Gradient profile, Whitby Town to Malton

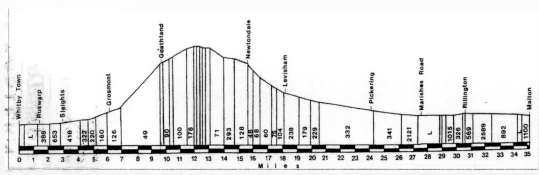

A PAST and PRESENT Companion

The
NORTH YORKSHIRE MOORS RAILWAY
Past and Present

John Hunt

Past & Present Publishing Ltd

British Library Cataloguing in Publication Data
A catalogue record for this book is available from the British Library.

Silver Link Publishing Ltd
The Trundle
Ringstead Road
Great Addington
Kettering
Northants NN14 4BW

Tel/Fax: 01536 330588

email: sales@nostalgiacollection.com

Website: www.nostalgiacollection.com

Printed and bound in the Czech Republic

ISBN   978 1 85895 290 1 (Softcover)
          978 1 85895 291 8 (Hardcover Limited Edition)

Acknowledgements

In preparing this book I am greatly indebted to the following photographers who have kindly made their 'past' pictures available: David Mitchell, Gavin Morrison, David Sutcliffe, John Spencer Gilks, Michael Mensing and Frank Dean. Thanks also to the Armstrong Trust for the pictures of John Boyes, and to Colour Rail for the pictures of C. Hogg and Jim Jarvis. I am also grateful to Nick Carter for supplying a wealth of historical NYMR pictures, together with details of those depicted – no mean task after 40-plus years! – and the other photographers who have submitted 'present' pictures. I also thank Mark Sissons, NYMR Archivist and Tamsyn Naylor, for checking the historical accuracy of the text, as well as helping to 'name names' in the photographs of people!

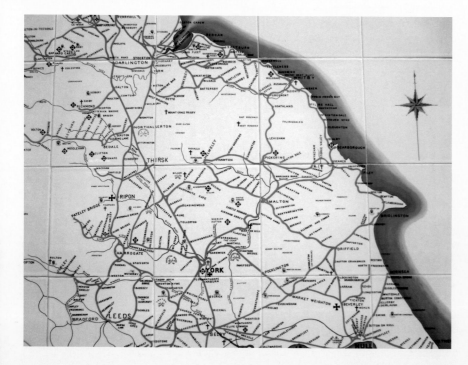

The NER tiled map that still adorns several stations on the former NER system, a new version of which was installed at Pickering in 2009.

Contents

LNER 'A4' 4-6-2 No 60007 *Sir Nigel Gresley* shunts its train at Whitby on 4 May 2008; in the background stands the Abbey. *JH*

Introduction

A Whitby to Pickering railway was proposed to connect the Vale of Pickering with the coast and improve the movement of goods both into and out of the area via the port of Whitby. The Royal Assent for the Whitby & Pickering Railway (W&PR) Act was received on 6 May 1833.

The northern terminus of the W&PR was at Whitby, and the first 'trains' – actually horse-drawn carriages – left there for Grosmont on 8 June 1835, with the line officially opening to Pickering on 26 May 1836, when it became only the third railway to open in Yorkshire.

In 1845 the W&PR became part of the York &

North Midland Railway (Y&NMR) and work began to convert the route from a horse-worked single line to a double track worked by steam locomotives. The line was connected to the growing national network when it was extended to Rillington Junction, east of Malton, on the York-Scarborough line, opening on 1 July 1845. The first steam-hauled train left Whitby via the newly opened route on 4 June 1847.

The Y&NMR was a founder member of the North Eastern Railway (NER) in 1854, but the new company regarded the steep rope-worked incline at Beckhole, between Grosmont and Goathland, to be a major hindrance. It therefore constructed a 4-mile diversionary line with easier gradients, which opened on 1 July 1865. On 2 October of that year the North Yorkshire & Cleveland Railway's line from Picton (between Eaglescliffe and Northallerton) via Castleton connected with the former W&PR at Grosmont.

Ten years later, on 1 April 1875, a single-line branch opened from Pickering westwards to Helmsley, and on 1 April 1882 the single-track Forge Valley line east from Pickering to Seamer was opened. In the same decade lines were opened from Whitby northwards along the coast to Loftus (3 December 1883), and south to Scarborough (16 July 1885); these lines accessed the original Whitby station via a spur from a new station at West Cliff, while the Scarborough line crossed the River Esk on the imposing Larpool Viaduct.

During the First World War the Whitby-Pickering line was singled between Levisham and New Bridge, just north of Pickering, the materials being utilised elsewhere to serve the war effort; the second track was never replaced.

The NER was swallowed up by the London & North Eastern Railway (LNER) at the 1923 Grouping, and the new company continued to operate all these lines until it was nationalised in 1948.

British Railways soon set about the task of rationalisation, even before the advent of the infamous Beeching Report. First to go was the truncated remains of the original route to Goathland, which had been retained between Beckhole and Deviation Junction at Grosmont. While part of it had been closed when a bridge was washed away in 1931, occasional goods trains served the hamlet of Esk Valley, which had no road access until 1951; the last train ran on 18 September of that year. Just prior to that, on 3 January 1950, the Forge Valley line closed, followed by the cessation of passenger services on the Helmsley route on 31 January 1953. Five years later, on 5 May 1958, the coastal route from Loftus to Whitby via Staithes was closed.

Then came Dr Beeching's report *The Re-shaping of British Railways*, published in March 1963, with its recommendations of wholesale closures across the UK. The routes to Whitby did not fare well. On 8 March 1965 the lines from Whitby to Scarborough and from Grosmont to Rillington Junction were closed, with only the Whitby-Middlesbrough line left to serve the harbour town. The section of line from New Bridge to Rillington Junction remained open for freight until it, too, succumbed on 1 July 1966.

The loss of the local lines led to widespread concerns, especially in the Goathland area, and thoughts turned to the possibility of reopening under private ownership. Matters came to a head when rumours abounded that track-lifting was imminent (there was an embargo on BR lifting track for two years following closure). This led to a meeting at Tom Salmon's house at Ruswarp on 3 June 1967, which was

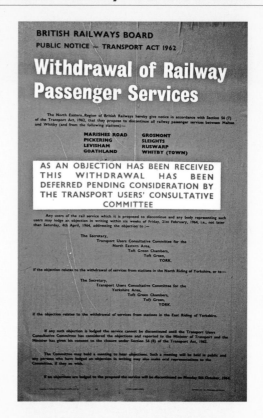

a precursor to the setting up of the North Yorkshire Moors Railway Preservation Society (NYMRPS) and its inaugural meeting at Goathland later that year on 18 November. Its aim was to reopen the 18-mile line from Grosmont to Pickering, both as a tourist railway and to preserve the rail link to Goathland, which was prone to being cut off by snow in winter. Negotiations started with BR to retain a single track throughout, but while these proceeded BR let a contract for the recovery of the second track between Grosmont and Levisham, and all of the track south of Pickering station. Working southwards, the track materials were taken out by train, with the final movement between Pickering and Rillington Junction taking place on 2 November 1969. The line was severed south of Pickering on the same day.

From 10 December 1968 volunteers were allowed access to the line, and rolling stock for the fledgling scheme started to arrive. The first was AC Cars railbus No W79978, which arrived at Grosmont on 9 August 1968, having travelled under its own power from Grangemouth in Scotland. The first steam locomotive to come to the railway was the diminutive Hudswell Clarke 0-4-0ST *Mirvale*, which was delivered by road for unloading in Pickering goods yard before steaming through to Grosmont on a snowy 2 February 1969. Nearly two months later, on 30 March, two more industrial steam locomotives – Borrows 0-4-0WT

No 3 and Andrew Barclay 0-6-0ST *Salmon* – arrived at Pickering and were also steamed through to Grosmont. From Easter 1970 it was possible for members to travel by steam train between Goathland and Summit, and later that year, on 25 June, the first BR steam locomotive – 'Q6' 0-8-0 No 63395 – arrived from Thornaby, via the Esk Valley line, together with former National Coal Board 0-6-2T No 29 from the extensive NCB system at Philadelphia in County Durham.

The NYMRPS evolved into the North Yorkshire Moors Historical Railway Trust in 1972. Following the granting of a Light Railway Order, which conveyed powers to operate the railway, public passenger services resumed at Easter 1973 between Grosmont and a temporary platform at High Mill, Pickering. The line was formally reopened by the Duchess of Kent on 1 May 1973 when she travelled by a Royal Train, headed by NER 'P3' 0-6-0 No 2392 and NCB 0-6-2T No 29, from Grosmont through to Pickering station. Initially services beyond Goathland were operated by a diesel multiple unit hired in from BR because there was as yet no access to the station at Pickering, and there was no locomotive run-round facility at High Mill. Eventually negotiations to secure Pickering station were successful and trains began operating along the full length of the line from 24 May 1975.

That year also saw limited steam operation on the Esk Valley line between Grosmont, Whitby and Battersby, as part of the Stockton & Darlington celebrations, and in subsequent years there were occasional forays onto the line to Whitby. However, the NYMR harboured visions of restoring regular through services from Pickering to Whitby by running its own trains over the 6 miles of Network Rail line between Grosmont and the town, and in 2007 the vision became reality when the railway secured its own safety case and passenger licence to meet Network Rail requirements. In 2014 it was possible to rebuild a second platform at Whitby, together with an engine release road, which had the combined effect of allowing an increase in the number of through trains to five a day and greatly simplified the process of locomotives running round their trains.

Fifty years on from the closure of the line from Grosmont to Rillington Junction, the North Yorkshire Moors Railway has come a very long way, a far cry from the modest ambitions of the early preservationists way back in 1967. It is now established as one of the premier heritage railways in the UK, with an annual turnover in excess of £5,000,000 and passenger numbers of more than 350,000 a year.

BR Standard 2-6-0 No 76079 leaves Whitby with a train for Pickering on 31 May 2011. *Dave Rodgers*

On 6 March 1965 the Stephenson Locomotive Society and Manchester Locomotive Society ran the 'Whitby Moors Rail Tour' from Manchester to Whitby. LMS 'Jubilee' 4-6-0 No 45698 *Mars* brought the train from Manchester to Wakefield Kirkgate, where LNER 'K4' 2-6-0 No 3442 *The Great Marquess* took over for the run to Market Weighton. Here LNER 'K1' 2-6-0 No 62005 was coupled inside the 'K4' for the run to Bridlington, Filey Holiday Camp, Scarborough Londesborough Road, Ravenscar and Whitby. At Prospect Hill Junction, the 'K4' was detached and drew the train down into Whitby Town, then the two locomotives headed the train to Grosmont, Goathland, Pickering, Malton and York, where the 'K1' was detached. This was the final BR steam train to traverse the line. Sadly, it was almost dark when the train reached Grosmont, but these pictures show the train during its journey. The first sees the two locomotives heading out of Staintondale, and the second the train on Larpool Viaduct, with the winter light fading. *Both Gavin Morrison*

Whitby

The town of Whitby dates back to around 650AD when a Benedictine monastery was established and a fishing port was developed. However, it was the coming of the railway that saw the town burgeon into a fashionable Victorian resort, marked by the development of West Cliff with substantial town houses and hotels.

This new-found grandeur was reflected in the railway station, built in 1847 to a design by G.T. Andrews, architect for the Y&NMR. Built in stone, it had two portico entrances, although the one on the Victoria Road frontage was just an architectural feature, only being opened up as an entrance in the 1930s. Originally the station had two platforms, but the opening of the additional lines to Middlesbrough, Loftus and Scarborough meant the addition of two further bay platforms, which were in use by 1884.

The station boasted a range of rooms for staff and passengers, but while most of the buildings have survived in alternative use – now Grade II listed – since the 1960s the various passenger facilities have been withdrawn. One notable survivor is the tiled map of the NER system. Comprising 64 white-based ceramic tiles, each 8 inches square, with title and brown border tiles, by 1910 these maps had been mounted on the walls of 23 principal stations, including Whitby.

Whitby Town had two signal boxes, one at the end of the platforms, adjacent to the goods shed, and the other at Bog Hall; the latter controlled the junction of the line up to Prospect Hill Junction and West Cliff station. Both closed on 30 September 1984 following the singling of the Esk Valley line and the removal of traditional signals.

On the west side of the line, opposite the Town signal box, was a two-road engine shed. Designed also by G.T. Andrews, it was 96 feet long but was extended to 200 feet in 1868. A 42-foot-diameter turntable was originally installed close to the shed, but was replaced by a larger example at Bog Hall in 1902. It was a very cramped site and locomotives were frequently stabled

WHITBY

This poster was issued by the LNER in around 1935, with artwork by K. Hauff. The photograph shows the comparable view on 3 November 2013. The swing bridge was erected in 1908; with a 75-foot span, it separates the upper and lower harbours. *Courtesy of National Railway Museum/JH*

in sidings on the opposite side of the running line. In 1955 Whitby received five brand-new BR Standard Class 4 2-6-4Ts, Nos 80116-20, and appropriately the boiler of No 80116 survives on the NYMR's No 80135. The shed closed on 6 April 1959, though the building still stands.

On the east side of the line was the goods yard and a large goods warehouse, again designed by G. T. Andrews. There was a total of nine sidings, which principally handled coal, fish and timber. Following the run-down of goods services and the withdrawal of facilities, the final pick-up freight between Whitby and Teesside ran on 2 May 1983. The site was subsequently redeveloped for car parking and the erection of a Co-op supermarket.

However, with the support of local authorities, national funding agencies, the Esk Valley Development Company and Network Rail, the NYMR rebuilt Platform 2 in 2013/14 and installed an engine release road between the two platforms; the new facility was formally opened on 12 August 2014.

In front of the eastern portico of Whitby station in 1964 is a priceless selection of period motor vehicles. The comparative, but uncluttered, view is from 13 March 2014. *Frank Dean/JH*

The view of Whitby station across the harbour is seen in 1962 and more than 50 years later, on 13 March 2014. Whilst the skyline has altered, some of the buildings to the right of the station remain clearly identifiable. A Tourist Information Centre now appears on the left. *David Sutcliffe/JH*

Platforms 1 and 2, seen in the 'past' view, were built in 1847, together with the overall roof, designed by G. T. Andrews. The internal supporting columns caused clearance problems, and the roof was removed in 1952/53. In the 'present' view LMS 'Black Five' 4-6-0 No 45428 *Eric Treacy* becomes the first locomotive to use the newly laid engine release road at Whitby on 4 August 2014, following the rebuilding of Platform 2. *Frank Dean collection/JH*

A Metro-Cammell DMU stands in Platform 2, forming the 3.50pm service to York on 26 February 1965. In a similar view on 4 August 2014, LMS 'Black Five' 4-6-0 No 45428 *Eric Treacy* is seen again about to run round its train. A Co-op supermarket stands on the site of Platforms 3 and 4, but many of the buildings on the skyline remain the same. *John Spencer Gilks/JH*

LNER 'B1' 4-6-0 No 61035 *Pronghorn* stands in Platform 1 with the 2.10pm Saturdays-only train to Leeds on 26 July 1958. On 31 October 2013 another 'B1', No 61264, waits to leave with the NYMR's 14.30 service to Pickering. *Michael Mensing/JH*

LNER 'K4' 2-6-0 No 3442 *The Great Marquess* backs onto its train, a BBC filming special from Leeds, on 13 April 1964. At the same location 50 years later unit No 156443 forms the 12.18 service to Middlesbrough on 25 September 2014. The houses on the left remain relatively unchanged, as do many of the buildings on the skyline. *John Spencer Gilks/JH*

Another 'B1' 4-6-0, No 61275, brings the 4.00pm train from Malton into Platform 2 some time in 1962; on the left are Platforms 3 and 4 and, behind the train, Whitby Town signal box. Built in 1884, the box was three storeys in height so that the signalman could see over the top of the goods shed. It closed on 30 September 1984, but parts were recovered for reuse by the NYMR, including bricks and architectural features that were used in the new signal box at Grosmont.

The comparative view shows LMS 'Black Five' 4-6-0 No 45428 *Eric Treacy* after arrival with the first NYMR train to use the new Platform 2 on 4 August 2014. The wall on the right, the planting boxes and houses on the skyline are common to both pictures. *John Spencer Gilks/JH*

This general view of the approach to Whitby Town on 9 June 1962 shows the locomotive shed on the left and the goods yard on the right. A line of covered vans stands in front of the goods shed, above which can be glimpsed the signal box.

The same view on 13 March 2014 graphically illustrates the rationalisation that has taken place; the goods yard is now a car park and, although the locomotive shed still stands, recent housing development precludes its use for that purpose again. *John Boyes/JH*

On 3 March 1965 No D6780 brings the Tees Yard-Whitby goods past Bog Hall signal box, while on 13 March 2014 unit No 156469 passes the same spot forming the 08.50 Whitby-Middlesbrough service.

Although the signal box has long gone (it also closed on 30 September 1984), the two tracks in the foreground remain, now the Bog Hall run-round loop, as does the public foot crossing. *Frank Dean/JH*

'B1' 4-6-0 No 61276 passes Bog Hall signal box with the 6.54pm train to Malton on 4 May 1964; on the right is the turntable, and beyond that the tidal estuary of the River Esk, with Whitby Abbey just visible to the right of the exhaust. In the 'present' picture, fellow 'B1' No 61264 is pictured in just the same spot on 31 October 2013 as it runs round its train in Bog Hall sidings. *John Boyes/JH*

Regular Whitby visitor 'B1' 4-6-0 No 61276 is turned on 14 May 1964. The 60-foot turntable was made by Cowans Sheldon in 1912 and was first used at York before being installed here in 1936; following the end of steam working it was removed in 1966.

The site is now part of the marina and no trace remains. No 61264 stands on the line furthest from the camera in the 'present' view, taken on 31 October 2013. The wall in the foreground, however, as well as some of the buildings in the background, are common to both pictures. *John Boyes/JH*

This panoramic view over Whitby, dominated by the Abbey, is dated 28 March 1962, and shows the turntable, carriage sidings, Bog Hall signal box and, just visible through the trees, the locomotive shed. Note, too, the half-cab bus.

In the present-day view, taken on 13 March 2014, gone are the signal box, turntable and sidings, the biggest change being reclamation of the estuary in 1979 to form a marina and public car park. *John Boyes/JH*

A DMU leaves Whitby for Middlesbrough in the summer of 1965. Following closure of the Scarborough line, the single-track link to Prospect Hill Junction, seen in the foreground, was no longer in use and the rails are rusty.

The comparative picture was taken from the overgrown trackbed of the former link and shows unit No 156469 forming the 12.18 service to Middlesbrough on 13 March 2014. The road bridge over the River Esk bypasses the congested town centre and its swing bridge, and was erected in 1980. *Frank Dean/JH*

No D6766, with the returning pick-up freight from Tees Yard, heads away from Whitby at Bog Hall on 14 May 1964. On the right is the spur up to Prospect Hill Junction and Whitby West Cliff.

In the present-day picture BR Standard 2-6-4T No 80135 brings the 08.15 NYMR service from Grosmont past the same location on 4 May 2003.

Later that day it would work two return trips to Glaisdale before returning to the NYMR. The track has been singled and the riverside footpath altered, but the retaining wall of the spur is still visible on the right. No 80135 carries the boiler from No 80116, which went new to Whitby shed in 1955. *John Boyes/JH*

Whitby to Grosmont

The line from Whitby to Grosmont opened in 1836 and was latterly double track after acquisition and rebuilding by the York & North Midland Railway in 1846/47. It followed the River Esk, crossing it no fewer than nine times in just over 5 miles. Soon after leaving Whitby, and hugging the northern bank of the River Esk, the line passes under Larpool Viaduct, by far the most impressive structure on the line; now carrying a footpath, the viaduct affords superb views of trains entering and leaving Whitby.

Now heading in a general south-westerly direction, the line serves intermediate stations at Ruswarp and Sleights. There was ironstone in the hills bounding the line and a number of sidings were also laid to serve the ironstone mines, but most had ceased production by the end of the 19th century.

Both Ruswarp and Sleights had small goods yards on the north side of the line, and both had signal boxes, the one at Sleights still extant in 2015. The goods facilities were withdrawn in 1983, though a coal business continued to occupy the yard at Sleights for some years afterwards. The signal boxes closed in September 1984 when the whole line from Whitby to Grosmont was singled, trains using the former down platform and up platform at the respective stations. The line from Grosmont to Whitby was then controlled from Nunthorpe using single-line token machines at Battersby, Glaisdale and Whitby, though in 2007 an intermediate token machine was also installed at Grosmont to facilitate through running between Whitby and Pickering.

LNER 'L1' 2-6-4T No 67766 approaches Ruswarp with the 7.50pm Whitby-Middlesbrough train on 23 July 1958. *Michael Mensing*

Larpool Viaduct dominates the scene as LNER 'K4' 2-6-0 No 3442 *The Great Marquess* brings the 'Whitby Moors Rail Tour' from Prospect Hill Junction down to Whitby Town on 6 March 1965. The train, double-headed by the 'K4' and LNER 'K1' 2-6-0 No 62005, had crossed the viaduct a few minutes earlier (see page 7).

A similar view at low tide in 1964 shows a DMU making its way out of Whitby alongside the River Esk.

The same view from the back road from Ruswarp to Whitby on 13 March 2014 is almost entirely obscured by trees. New housing has appeared on The Batts to the left, and the gas works on the right is long gone; opened in 1871, it closed in 1960. *John Spencer Gilks/Frank Dean/JH*

Construction of Larpool Viaduct commenced in October 1882 and it was opened in 1885; costing £40,000, it was 915 feet long, used 5 million bricks and carried a single track across 13 arches at a height of 125 feet above the River Esk. Following closure of the Scarborough line and abandonment of the idea of retaining the track as far as Hawsker in the event of potash mining in the area, the viaduct was fenced off. It survived a threat of demolition in 1989 and now carries a public coastal footpath – The Cinder Track – linking Whitby and Scarborough. In the 'past' picture an LNER 'A8' 4-6-2T heads a Whitby-Malton train on 8 May 1958, while on 3 November 2013 LMS 4-6-0 No 45428 *Eric Treacy* heads the 14.00 Whitby-Pickering service; the growth of lineside vegetation precludes a direct comparison. *C. Hogg, Colour Rail/JH*

LNER 'L1' 2-6-4T No 67766 is seen again, approaching Ruswarp with the 7.50pm Whitby-Middlesbrough train on 24 July 1958. On 10 September 2014 LNER 'B1' 4-6-0 No 61264 (masquerading as No 61034 *Chiru*) is in the same location with the 14.30 Whitby-Pickering service. Common to both pictures is the house, just discernible at the rear of the train. However, half a century of tree growth now hides Larpool Viaduct. *Michael Mensing/JH*

On 14 May 1964 LNER 'B1' 4-6-0 No 61018 *Gnu* stands at Ruswarp ready to shunt wagons from the 6.45am York-Whitby pick-up freight into the goods yard on the right. In contrast, on 13 March 2014 unit No 156469 leaves with the 07.04 Middlesbrough-Whitby service. Gone is the second track, platform and goods yard, but the building above the concrete shed on the right can be glimpsed behind the trees. *John Boyes/JH*

Looking west, Ruswarp station is in immaculate condition on 9 August 1966, while in the present-day view, taken on 13 March 2014, gone are the signals, signal box, up platform and beautifully tended gardens. The station house, however, remains in good order, now privately occupied. *Frank Dean/JH*

LNER 'B1' 4-6-0 No 61319 crosses the River Esk at Ruswarp with the 6.45am York-Whitby goods on 25 May 1964. Class 156 unit No 156469 is at the same spot on 13 March 2014, forming the 10.28 Middlesbrough-Whitby service. In the intervening years the up line has been removed, as has the segregated walkway over the bridge, and, in the background, Sneaton Sidings. The sidings were constructed in 1898 to serve the livestock market (still there today), but were closed on 2 August 1965. *John Boyes/JH*

Two three-car Metro-Cammell DMUs leave Sleights in the spring of 1964 bound, according to the rear destination blind, for Scarborough, which will involve a reversal at Whitby. The corresponding present-day view is of unit No 156444 forming the 10.28 Middlesbrough-Whitby service on 15 April 2014. The down-side waiting shelter was recovered by the NYMR in 1989 and now serves as the booking office at Grosmont station. While the goods yard is now disused and overgrown, the signal box still stands. *John Spencer Gilks/JH*

Viewed from the 1930 bridge that carries the main A169 Pickering-Whitby road, LNER 'K4' 2-6-0 No 3442 *The Great Marquess* approaches Sleights with the BBC filming special from Leeds to Whitby on 13 April 1964. the same location, and almost exactly 50 years later, the same locomotive heads the 'Esk Valley Explorer' railtour from York to Whitby on 22 March 2014. *David Mitchell/JH*

LNER 'B1' 4-6-0 No 61319 is seen once again approaching Sleights with the 6.45am York-Whitby goods on 25 May 1964. The comparative view depicts unit No 156444 as the 10.28 Middlesbrough-Whitby service on 15 April 2014. *John Boyes/JH*

LNER 'G5' 0-4-4T No 67343 leaves Sleights at Easter 1954 with a Whitby-Malton train. From a similar viewpoint, but with the 1930 road bridge in the background, LMS 4-6-0 No 45428 *Eric Treacy* accelerates away from Sleights with the 14.30 Whitby-Pickering service on 3 November 2013. *Jim Jarvis, Colour Rail/JH*

This 1964 view, looking east, shows in the distance Eskdale or Birtley Mines signal box. The 'present' picture shows the same view on 13 March 2014.

The bridge, with its sloping handrails, is instantly recognisable. *Frank Dean/JH*

Grosmont

The settlement of Grosmont dates from the 13th century, but it was the discovery of ironstone during the building of the railway in 1833 that caused the village to expand. In 1862 two blast furnaces were built to smelt the local ironstone, a third furnace being added in 1876, but the ironworks closed in 1891. Ironstone from bigger and better mines in Cleveland to the north, together with foreign imports, led to the decline of mining in the Grosmont area, and by 1915 the final mine had closed. There is little evidence of the former mining industry today, and the wooded ironworks site is now a National Park car park. Opposite the ironworks site, however, lie the still recognisable remains of the brickworks, established in the 1860s but closed in 1957.

The Station Inn, adjacent to the station and originally named the Tunnel Inn, was built in 1835 to provide accommodation for the Whitby & Pickering Railway (W&PR). Next to it, the old Post Office was originally a W&PR goods warehouse, with stables behind. Another reminder of the W&PR is the suspension footbridge over the Murk Esk, which was built in 1858 to replace the original wooden bridge. Just south of the suspension bridge lies the original tunnel for the first horse-drawn trains. It is 120 yards long and was built using stone from the nearby Lease Rigg quarry; the castellated portals are particularly noteworthy. The York & North Midland Railway built the adjacent, larger two-track tunnel in 1845, together with a single-span double-track stone bridge over the river, as part of its conversion of the line from horse to locomotive haulage. The original tunnel now provides pedestrian access to the NYMR's locomotive depot.

On 2 October 1865 Grosmont became a junction with the opening of the North Yorkshire & Cleveland Railway's single line from Picton and Middlesbrough, and it was this line that was reprieved from closure.

Since 1967, under the auspices of the NYMR, the station area has steadily been developed and now has four platforms, making it one of the largest, in terms of numbers of platforms, in Yorkshire! To achieve this, the original up platform was made into an island platform and the old down platform was extended northwards to accommodate the NYMR's longest trains; this meant slewing the Esk Valley line to accommodate the extension.

The original signal box that controlled the junction was dismantled in 1980, the top finding a new use at Alston on the South Tynedale Railway. A new box, adjacent to the level crossing, was commissioned in 1996, and incorporated items from a number of similar North East signal boxes, including Whitby Town and Horden.

A new footbridge, connecting Platforms 1 and 2 to the ironworks site car park, came from the Kent & East Sussex Railway and was erected in 1990. The booking office came from Sleights, but otherwise most of the station buildings are original, though now put to new uses, such as a tea room. There is a shop in the 1846 station house, the rest of which is available as a holiday let.

South of Grosmont Tunnel lies the depot and workshops for the NYMR's fleet of steam and diesel locomotives. Initially developed in 1972, when the first shed was erected, the site has grown incrementally over subsequent years.

The classic F. M. Sutcliffe photograph of Grosmont ironworks, taken in about 1889.

The reopening Royal Train stands outside Grosmont station, ready to pick up its Royal guest, the Duchess of Kent, on 1 May 1973. The train had special dispensation to run from Whitby itself, but a national railway strike that day prevented this, the Duchess travelling by limousine from Whitby to Grosmont. The first view was taken from the signal box, and also shows the brickworks remains.

The comparative view was taken from the footbridge in March 2001, and shows the extended Platform 2, the slewed Esk Valley line, the new connection close to the overbridge (since demolished) and the water column from Derwenthaugh, erected in 1991. Ex-NCB 0-6-2T No 29 brings empty carriages into the station from the sidings in the distance. The connection to the NR Esk Valley line can be seen passing through the gap in the fence beyond the water column. *Both JH*

In May 1976 a BR engineer's train bound for Battersby, headed by a Class 47 diesel, became derailed just beyond Platform 1. The NYMR's Yorkshire Engine Co 0-4-0 diesel shunter propels two Hull & Barnsley Railway open wagons, loaded with packing timber, onto the Esk Valley line to assist in the rerailing.

The comparative view is much changed, with the slewing of the Esk Valley line, the extension of Platform 2 and the addition of the footbridge. However, the house gable visible to the right of the signal box and through the footbridge in the modern picture is a constant feature. *Both JH*

LNER 'B1' 4-6-0 No 61018 *Gnu*, heading the 6.45am York-Whitby goods, shunts the goods yard at Grosmont on 14 May 1964; the yard was in the 'V' of the junction of the Pickering and Middlesbrough lines. The signal box was a North Eastern Railway S2 design, erected in 1908. Its proximity to the BR line and remoteness from the level crossing meant that it could not be realistically reused by the NYMR, so it was dismantled in 1980, the wooden top going to the South Tynedale Railway at Alston.

The same viewpoint on 10 September 2014 is somewhat different! The building on the extreme left, now the tea room, is in both pictures, but the platform has been extended, the building in the centre is the one from Sleights, and the footbridge on the right came from the K&ESR. *John Boyes/JH*

The signalman waits to give the single-line token as LNER 'B1' 4-6-0 61031 *Reedbuck* arrives at Grosmont's Platform 3 with the RCTS/SLS 'North Eastern Tour' on 1 October 1963 (it had arrived from Malton behind No 61021 *Reitbok* and was en route to Battersby and Northallerton).

Looking from virtually the same spot 50 years later, unit No 156451 arrives at Grosmont forming the 12.18 Whitby-Middlesbrough service on 7 November 2013. *David Mitchell/JH*

This rather desolate scene at Grosmont station, despite the sun shining, is looking south towards the tunnel on 7 September 1968. The NYMR's first item of rolling stock, AC Cars railbus No W79978, stands beyond the level crossing gates, having arrived from Grangemouth the previous month.

In the comparative view, taken 46 years later almost to the day, on 10 September 2014, much has changed. Both platforms have been extended northwards, the up platform, on the left, losing its brick wall and becoming an island. The signalling has proliferated to control the additional moves now possible, and the new signal box can be seen above the platform building on the left. *Alan Brown/JH*

In a view looking north from the south end of Grosmont Tunnel in 1964, the level crossing gates and the signal box can be glimpsed through the bore. On the right are Tunnel Cottages, occupied by railway workers but later used by NYMR staff and volunteers until demolished to make way for shed extensions. The bushes mark the site of an old turntable.

The 'present' view, taken from almost the same point on 31st May 2011, gives an indication of how much the site has subsequently been developed. Part of the repair shed is visible between the two locomotives, which are new-build LNER 'A1' 4-6-2 No 60163 *Tornado* and BR Standard 2-6-0 No 76079; the latter sits beneath the mechanical coaling plant, built in 1998 and the only one of its kind in the UK. *David Sutcliffe/David Rodgers*

The first repair shed to be erected, commenced in 1972, can be seen in the background of this picture from the summer of 1973, which shows volunteers laying a turnout to provide a second road into the shed. By the tunnel stands LNER 'Q6' 0-8-0 No 3395 and Fowler 0-4-0DM shunter No 21, while in the shed is RSH 0-4-0ST No 15 *Eustace Forth*; both the 0-4-0s had left the railway by 1980.

In the present-day picture, taken on 7 November 2013, the same turnout is in the foreground and the portal frame shed in the earlier picture is the one with the brick facade in the modern one. In front of it, roads 2 and 3 comprise the fabrication shop dating from 1996, while behind it, to the right, can be glimpsed the roof of the two-road running shed built in 1990, with the oil store in front of it. *Both JH*

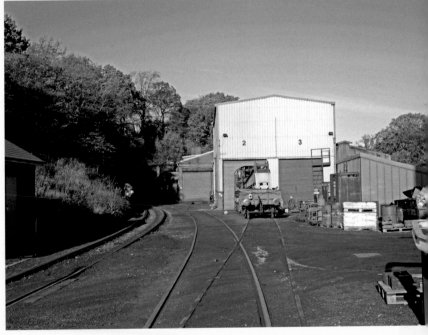

Grosmont to Goathland

From Grosmont the line runs for 3½ miles to Goathland, and most of it, from Deviation to just short of Goathland's platforms, is at an unbroken climb of 1 in 49. Passing the locomotive depot, Deviation shed stands on the left, on the site of Deviation signal box. This was built in 1865 and controlled the junction of the Grosmont Old branch, also referred to as the Beckhole branch, with the 1865 diversionary route, which replaced the rope-worked incline between Beckhole and Goathland. The branch was latterly cut back to Esk Valley Cottages until closure in 1951. The box survived out of use and was utilised for volunteer accommodation for a time before demolition to make way for the three-road Deviation shed in 1977. This shed came from the Longmoor Military Railway at Liss, Hampshire, and was re-erected in 1979 by the North Eastern Locomotive Preservation Group. The old 1836 route is now a

difficulties exaggerated by adverse weather and very poor road access, were successfully overcome.

Beyond Water Ark, the line passes Darnholm, a favourite spot for train-watching and picnicking, and crosses the Eller Beck again before the final climb into Goathland.

The new bridge at Water Ark being lifted into place on 11 February 2010. *JH*

No 63395 rounds Darnholm curve with a goods train on 26 September 2014. *Robin Patrick*

popular walkway between Grosmont and Goathland.

The line traverses the eastern side of the valley of the Murk Esk as far as Beckhole, then follows the Eller Beck, a tributary of the Murk Esk. It crosses the Eller Beck no fewer than three times in quick succession at Thomasson Foss and Water Ark; the first two bridges are single stone arches, but the third, at Water Ark, was an iron girder span; considered to be life-expired, the latter was replaced between January and March 2010 in an ambitious project, where logistical

In the first view, 1898-built Borrows 0-4-0WT No 3, from Wallsend Slipway, in the care of the Newcastle University Railway Society (and carrying the University crest in front of the chimney), hauls a Hull & Barnsley Railway coach at Green End on 27 March 1969, the first NYMR 'passenger' train to run between Grosmont and Goathland. No 3 left the railway in 1981 and is now on the Tanfield Railway.

Just after it arrived on the NYMR, following restoration on Teesside, the North Eastern Locomotive Preservation Group's NER 'P3' 0-6-0 No 2392 is seen on its inaugural run from Grosmont to Goathland on 25 October 1971.

Similarly viewed from the top of a concrete PW cabin, in October 1998 LNER 'K1' 2-6-0 No 62005, also owned by the NELPG, passes the same location with a Grosmont-Pickering train. The 'K1' came to the NYMR in June 1974 after overhaul at Thornaby. *John Boyes/JH (2)*

LNER 'A8' 4-6-2T No 69861 climbs the 1 in 49 at Beckhole with a Whitby-Malton train at Easter 1954, while on 31 May 2013 LNER 'B1' 4-6-0 No 61264, temporarily renumbered as 61002 *Impala*, passes the same spot with the 09.00 Whitby-Pickering service. *Jim Jarvis, Colour Rail/JH*

LNER 'B1' 4-6-0 No 61337 heads a Whitby-Malton train across Thomasson Foss bridge, unique in that it has a footbridge beneath it, also crossing the Eller Beck. Fifty years later, another 'B1', No 61264, masquerading as No 61034 *Chiru*, crosses the same bridge with the 09.30 Grosmont-Pickering service on 11 July 2014. *David Sutcliffe/JH*

In the summer of 1964 an unidentified LMS 'Black Five' heads up the 1 in 49 at Darnholm with a Whitby-Leeds train, while in May 1981 Clayton No

D8568 passes the same spot with a Grosmont-Pickering service. *David Sutcliffe/JH*

LMS 2-6-4T No 42085 heads the 3.14pm Whitby-Malton train at Darnholm on 25th July 1958. The present equivalent picture shows LMS 'Black Five'

4-6-0 No 44806 passing the same spot with the 12.30 Grosmont-Pickering 'Moorlander' dining train on 1 November 2014. *Michael Mensing/JH*

Goathland village is 500 feet above sea level, with a population of around 430, and has a history extending from Viking times. In 1109 King Henry I granted land to Osmund the priest and brethren of the hermitage of Goathland, then called Godelandia, for the soul of his mother Queen Matilda, who had died in 1083; this is recorded in a charter held at Whitby Abbey. The village was a spa resort in the 19th century.

Much of the surrounding land is owned by the Duchy of Lancaster, and the Duchy's tenants have a common right, extending for hundreds of years, to graze their black-faced sheep on the village green and surrounding moorland.

Latterly, Goathland's claim to fame has been its starring role in the hit television series *Heartbeat*, set in the 1960s and running to no fewer than 18 series between 1992 and 2010. Many of the scenes were shot on the NYMR and at Goathland station.

The 1836 railway actually ran just to the north of the present Goathland public house, and over much of its length is now a public footpath. When the 1865 deviation was built, a new station, initially known as Goathland Mill, was opened on the eastern edge of the village. Remarkably, the station and its associated buildings have changed little since they were built, and the view from the neighbouring Cow Wath bridge (also known as Barnet House bridge) is much the same today is it was more than a century ago.

One notable change, however, has been the disappearance of the old stone-crusher and loading facility on the up side, behind the present water tank. Dating from the latter part of the 19th century, Whinstone was mined on the moors above Goathland and brought to the station via the Sil Howe tramway, then loaded onto rail wagons via a stone-crusher. This was powered by a Pelton Wheel from 1936 until the mines closed in 1951. Little trace remains today, though NYMR volunteers recovered the remains of the Pelton Wheel in 1969 and used it for a time to generate electricity for the first volunteer accommodation coach at Goathland.

In the early days of the NYMR Goathland was the headquarters of the Preservation Society, and was where the first rolling stock was based and maintained, including the railbus and the first steam locomotives, *Mirvale*, *Salmon* and No 3. They were joined by 'Q6' No 63395 and NCB No 29 in 1970, and No 5 and 'P3' No 2392 in 1971, but by then the motive power department had been formed and moved down to its present site at Grosmont.

In the preservation era the station has not only been transformed to its former glory but also considerably enhanced, without detracting from its character, to represent a typical NER station circa 1922. The goods warehouse has been converted into an award-winning tea room, retaining its wooden loading platform and hand crane, with customers seated in two Hull & Barnsley Railway open wagons. To cater for the vastly increased number of passengers now visiting Goathland station, a footbridge, from Howdon on Tyneside, was erected in 1984, and a camping coach for public hire was introduced in the 1990s, continuing a tradition going back to 1932, when the LNER installed camping coaches at Goathland – and Grosmont – and perpetuated by BR between 1961 and 1964. Also carrying on a long-standing tradition is railway occupancy of the station house, now by NYMR employees. The house, designed by Thomas Prosser and dating from 1865, has changed little over the intervening years.

At Goathland station, looking south, on 30 June 1972, the growing collection of rolling stock can be glimpsed in the up and down sidings reinstated by NYMR volunteers, with the AC Cars railbus visible by the up starting signal. In the distance is Cow Wath bridge.

Seventeen years later, in July 1989, GWR 0-6-2T No 6619 takes water with a down train from Pickering. The station is looking much more cared for, and the buildings having received a different colour scheme. *David Idle/JH*

On 13 April 1964 LNER 'K4' 2-6-0 No 3442 *The Great Marquess* waits in the station with the BBC filming train from Leeds to Whitby. The second view, from the winter of 1964, shows a two-car Metro-Cammell DMU calling in the station with a Malton-Whitby working.

Goathland was used by Warner Brothers for filming sequences for the first 'Harry Potter' film, *Harry Potter and the Philosopher's Stone*, released in 2001. The third picture shows GWR 'Hall' 4-6-0 No 5972 *Olton Hall*, masquerading as *Hogwarts Castle*, standing in the station during filming. *David Mitchell (2)/JH*

A desolate Goathland station, devoid of sidings and with the signal box boarded up, is seen during the winter of 1967/68. In a far more healthy scene 40 years later, on 19 March 2007, NCB 0-6-2T No 29 stands in the station with a Grosmont-Pickering train. Prior to ownership by the NCB, No 29 was operated by the Lambton Hetton & Joicey Colliery Company, hence 'LH&JC' on the tank sides. *P. Walton/JH*

In the 'past' picture, when Goathland was the base for the locomotives, LNER 0-8-0 'Q6' No 3395, another NELPG engine, stands in the up platform while *Mirvale*, *Salmon* and NCB 0-6-2T No 5 are prepared in the relaid up sidings on 30 August 1970.

A few years later, in July 1976, LNER 'J52' 0-6-0ST No 1247 has just taken water after bringing its train up from Grosmont, and is about to swap with hired-in BR Class 08 0-6-0 diesel shunter No 08212 for the onward journey to Levisham. *David Idle/JH*

The classic view of Goathland station is to be obtained from Cow Wath bridge. In the first scene, dating from August 1969, the signal box has been opened up, signal arms replaced and two of the three original down sidings have been relaid. In one of them stands the AC Cars railbus No W79968, still in its BR livery.

On 25 June 1970 NCB 0-6-2T No 29 is engaged in the shunting of three coaches and Andrew Barclay 0-6-0ST *Salmon*, while on the left the siding to the goods shed has been partially relaid. The railbus is in the throes of repainting from its previous BR livery into the LNER tourist livery of green and cream.

Finally, LMS 'Black Five' 4-6-0 No 44806 pauses with the NYMR's prestige 'Moorlander' luncheon dining train on 1 November 2014. Like Levisham, Goathland's passing loop allows the crossing of up and down trains. Note that the down siding has been extended as far as the goods shed and now houses the NYMR's demonstration goods train. *P. Walton/JH (2)*

During the NELPG's fifth anniversary celebrations, NER 'P3' 0-6-0 No 2392 leaves for the Summit on 20 November 1971. In the corresponding 'present' view, BR Standard 4-6-0 No 75029 *The Green Knight* heads for Pickering on 23 February 2013. *Chris Gammell/JH*

On 5 March 1965 a Metro-Cammell DMU from Whitby reverses before its return journey at 12.59. In a similar location on 26 October 2011 GWR 'Manor' 4-6-0 No 7822 *Foxcote Manor* leaves for Pickering. The view has changed little, except for the erection of the impressive three-way bracket signal, which is made up of parts from signals at Redmarshall, Glaisdale and Bridlington. The 21 milepost and the petrol trolley shed are the same in both pictures. *Frank Dean/JH*

Leaving Goathland, the line leaves the narrow valley of the Eller Beck and climbs more gradually onto the moors and to the summit of the line 589 feet above sea level. En route, on the west side of the line, the original 1836 formation can be seen, the two formations joining at Moorgates, where two York & North Midland Railway houses and a stone overbridge mark the course of the original line. Approaching the highest point on the line, the remains of Goathland Summit signal box can be seen on the left, before the line crosses the Lyke Wake Walk, a 42-mile path across the North York Moors from Osmotherly in the west to Robin Hoods Bay in the east. Goathland Summit was the destination of the early members' trains that ran in the early 1970s from Goathland.

The line now crosses the watershed at Fen Bog, a marshy area even today, which caused the original railway builders to 'float' the line by pile-driving fir trees into the bog and overlaying them with sheaves of heather bound in sheepskin, together with more timber and moss, a technique Stephenson had used on Chat Moss in Lancashire. High up to the left, beyond the main Pickering-Whitby road, stands the RAF's Fylingdales early warning station, once characterised by the 'giant golfballs'!

The line now falls first into Northdale, then Newtondale, glacial overflow channels dating from the Ice Age. In Northdale the line passes the ruins of Carter's House on the right, once used for stabling horses. This part of the line, inaccessible by public roads, is perhaps the most attractive because of its remoteness; on alighting at Newtondale Halt, which was opened on 23 April 1981, once the train has departed an eerie silence can descend into the valley.

Beyond the Halt, where Newtondale signal box once stood (only the foundations on the left-hand side can be seen today), the line falls at 1 in 49 for a distance, a reminder that, in parts, the northbound climb is just as taxing as the southbound climb from Grosmont. Up on the valley sides can be glimpsed Skelton Tower, a two-storey tower built around 1830 as a shooting lodge by a former rector of Levisham, the Reverend Robert Skelton. Some say that he wrote his sermons in the lodge, but it is also rumoured that he escaped there to enjoy a quiet drink!

Shortly the line reaches Raindale, where The Grange, formerly the Raindale Inn, on the right, was also used for stabling horses used on the original railway.

BR Standard 4-6-0 No 75029 *The Green Knight* runs amidst the autumnal colours of Newtondale with the 11.20 Pickering-Grosmont train on 30 October 2007. Skelton Tower is just visible above the rear of the train. JH

A few days before the line's closure, a DMU forming the 14.20 Malton-Whitby service passes Moorgates on 5 March 1965, while in the second picture No D7628 heads the 12.30 Grosmont-Pickering train on 2 January 2014. Despite the gap of nearly 50 years between the two pictures, the trees on the left are recognisable, as are the overhead line posts, though the tree on the right has recently succumbed to old age! *Frank Dean/JH*

This pair of cottages at Moorgates was designed by G. T. Andrews for the York & North Midland Railway and built in 1845; originally accommodating the level-crossing keepers, the cottages became obsolete with the opening of the deviation line in 1865. They are still occupied and are Grade II listed. Interestingly, they still retain the old sleeper fences. In both pictures, the 1836 line can be seen to the right (leading from the gate in the 'present' picture), with the 1865 deviation beyond that. The past picture was taken on 5 March 1965 and the other on 15 April 2014. *Frank Dean/JH*

An unidentified LMS 'Black Five' 4-6-0 heads a Whitby-Leeds train at Eller Beck in the spring of 1963. On the opposite side of the line above the beck can be seen the road leading to Goathland village.

In the formative years of the embryonic NYMR, the second picture shows Andrew Barclay 0-6-0ST *Salmon* propelling a Thompson CL coach from Goathland to the Summit in March 1970.

At the same location on 12 March 2008 LNER 'A4' 4-6-2 No 60007 *Sir Nigel Gresley*, flagship locomotive on the modern NYMR, hauls a matching rake of 'blood and custard' Mark 1 coaches. *David Sutcliffe/John Boyes/JH*

Looking in the opposite direction at Eller Beck, a Metro-Cammell DMU coasts downhill with a Malton-Whitby service in the late summer of 1963.

On 20 November 1971 the NELPG marked its fifth anniversary by running its two locomotives, No 2392 and LNER 'Q6' 0-8-0 No 3395 on goods and passenger trains. Here the 'Q6' runs back from Summit with the goods train.

On 4 June 1983 'Deltic' No 55009 *Alycidon* heads north with a Pickering-Grosmont train. On the left horizon can be seen the erstwhile 'giant golfballs', or radomes, of RAF Fylingdales. *David Sutcliffe/JH (2)*

Goathland Summit signal box is seen in the late summer of 1963, by which time it had been taken out of use and, while the signal posts remain, they are devoid of arms. The present-day picture, dated 28 February 1971, shows NCB 0-6-2T No 5 on a works train. *David Sutcliffe/Chris Gammell*

LNER 'B1' 4-6-0 No 61021 *Reitbok*, with its steam-operated sanders still on after the climb from Levisham, approaches the Lyke Wake Walk crossing at Fen Bog with the RCTS/SLS 'North Eastern Tour' on 1 October 1963.

Half a century later, and seen from the same vantage point, fellow 'B1' No 61264 brings a train from Pickering to Grosmont on 14 November 2013. Other than the removal of the second track and some lineside bush growth, not much has changed. *David Mitchell/JH*

Further south from the Lyke Wake Walk crossing, another but unidentified 'B1' brings the short 4.08pm Malton-Whitby train across Fen Bog in the autumn of 1961. In the corresponding 'present' picture, LNER 'Q6' 0-8-0 No 63395 heads a short northbound goods train on 7 November 2007. *David Sutcliffe/JH*

The second day of February 1969 was an auspicious day for the infant NYMR as it saw the first steam locomotive movement since the 'Whitby Moors Rail Tour' of 6 March 1965. Hudswell Clarke 0-4-0ST *Mirvale* was steamed through from Pickering to Grosmont, and is seen here crossing Fen Bog. Twenty-eight years later BR Standard 4-6-0 No 75014 is seen in the same location on a Grosmont-Pickering train in January 1997. *Both JH*

Viewed across the expanse of Fen Bog, an unidentified 'B1' leads its four-coach Whitby-Malton train into Northdale in the summer of 1963. In virtually the same spot LNER 'J52' 0-6-0ST No 1247 brings a five-coach train out of Northdale in July 1979. *David Sutcliffe/JH*

In the heart of Northdale, LNER 'B1' No 61319 heads the 4.08pm Malton-Whitby train in the summer of 1964, conveying, at the front, two through coaches that had left London King's Cross at 11.30am; the rear vehicle is a Thompson centre lavatory composite coach. Passing the very same spot on 15 April 2014 is 'B1' No 61264 with the 14.00 Pickering-Grosmont service. *David Sutcliffe/JH*

Another, but unknown, 'B1' brings the lightweight 4.08pm Malton-Whitby train into Northdale in the spring of 1963, while in the same place on 10

November 2013 BR 4-6-0 No 75029 *The Green Knight* heads a Pickering-Grosmont luncheon service. *David Sutcliffe/JH*

Levisham

Levisham station can hardly be regarded as convenient, since it lies 1½ miles from and 300 feet lower than the settlement it purports to serve! However, there is a reason for this; the location of the station was influenced by the local landowner and Lord of the Manor, the Reverend Robert Skelton. A station built at Farwath, 1½ miles closer to Pickering, would have been more convenient for the surrounding villages of Levisham, Lockton and Newton-on-Rawcliffe, but the Rev Skelton built a property, Grove House, and, wanting the station next to it, provided the land where the present station was built.

The station house pre-dates the opening of the railway and was converted from a farmhouse around 1845-47 by architect G. T. Andrews, which may explain why it stands at an angle to the platform. Adjacent to the station house stand two former platelayers' cottages built in 1858. Constructed to a North Eastern Railway design, six were built on the Whitby and Pickering branch at the same time; they did not receive electricity until the 1980s!

During the NYMR years, facilities at the station have gradually been improved. New sidings have been laid, one of which has accommodated a camping coach since 2004, as at Goathland perpetuating a long LNER and BR tradition. Following singling of the line in 1969, it became necessary to provide a passing loop in the station, and this meant installation of a turnout at the north end of the station in 1975. The loop was subsequently extended at the south end to accommodate ten-coach trains with two locomotives.

Controlled from the original 1876 signal box, the station has been fully signalled using mainly slotted-post lower-quadrant types as used by the NER in this area and in keeping with the 1912 period feel of the station. The level crossing has been resurfaced and the traditional wooden gates have given way to automatic barriers and flashing lights to meet modern-day requirements. Finally, a new, longer siding was laid north of the level crossing, parallel with the running line.

Other developments have seen a new weighbridge building, complete with weigh table, recovered from Wadsley Bridge, and used as a catering establishment called Weighbridge Teas, while in the station house the railway's artist in residence, Chris Ware, has a studio. South of the station house lies a paddock, which is regularly used for special events and usually sports a marquee. Vintage vehicles, 1960s music, real ale festivals and wartime weekend events are popular attractions at Levisham.

LNER 'V2' 2-6-2 No 4771 *Green Arrow* leaves Levisham northbound on 14 March 2008. *JH*

The transformation at Levisham: in September 1972, while the railbus is attracting attention from a few onlookers, the station has yet to receive the improvements that are readily apparent in the more recent view, taken on 10 November 2013. Gone are the weeds, while a passing loop, with attendant signalling, has been installed, and a down siding laid. *Nigel Trotter/JH*

A volunteer working party loads track materials onto the trailer of a Wickham trolley on the northern approach to Levisham station in June 1974. These vehicles played an essential role in the early days of the NYMR, especially in the days before regular works trains could operate. In a similar location, BR 'Western' Class 52 No D1048 *Western Lady* accelerates out of the station with a Pickering-Grosmont train in June 1979. *Both JH*

Looking very well cared for, especially in the floral department, the station is well manicured in the first view, taken on 14 August 1961. Not a lot has changed by the date of the 'present' picture, taken on 24 April 2008. New and resited signals have appeared and the road crossing has been upgraded. Since this picture was taken the Levisham Station Group has rebuilt an exact copy of the lamp room that appears on the up platform in the 1961 view. *David Sutcliffe/JH*

In September 1999 two scrap trains ran from Teesside to New Bridge yard at Pickering for loading, then went on to Liverpool. On 10 September the second train, with EWS No 66055 hauling seven empty MBA wagons, arrives at Levisham.

The 'present' view shows LMS 'Black Five' 4-6-0 No 44806 at exactly the same place with 'The Moorlander' dining train from Grosmont to Pickering on 1 November 2014. *Both JH*

This is Levisham as it appeared in 1964, with a Whitby-Malton DMU arriving from the north. Compare this with the view 50 years later from the same vantage point (with the signaller and driver's cooperation!), as BR Class 37 No 37264 arrives on 10 September 2014. Afforestation has altogether altered the appearance of the bare hillsides, the slope of the platform ramps has been eased, and the siding to the small goods yard has been completely remodelled and relaid further to the south. *David Sutcliffe/JH*

LNER 'B1' 4-6-0 No 61002 *Impala* passes through the station en route from Whitby to York on 2 March 1965. The photographer tells the tale that shunting the return pick-up goods at Whitby had been delayed to such an extent that the locomotive crew, concerned about their hours – and no doubt also the weather – decided to leave the goods behind and return to York light engine!

In the present-day view, LMS 'Black Five' 4-6-0 No 45407, masquerading as No 45157 *The Glasgow Highlander*, enters the station with a Grosmont-Pickering train in October 2003. *Frank Dean/JH*

In the first view an LMS 'Black Five' 4-6-0 heads north out of Levisham with a Malton-Whitby train in September 1964. Ten years later, from a slightly different vantage point, another 'Black Five', No 5428 *Eric Treacy*, propels the BR weed-killing train out of the station on 6 May 1974. *Frank Dean/JH*

Levisham to Pickering

The line from Levisham to New Bridge, Pickering, was, like the rest of the 1865 route, double track, but in 1917 one of the tracks was lifted for the war effort and never replaced. From Levisham to Farwath the line is dead straight for 1½ miles, most of which was the subject of a complete relaying by the NYMR in the winter of 2013/14. At the time it was believed to be the longest such relaying completed in one go on any standard-gauge heritage railway.

Much of the line passes through land that belongs to the Duchy of Lancaster, most of it forested, and there is no public road access to the line until New Bridge. Just before that point, at Hunting Bridge, the Environment Agency has carried out extensive groundworks to alleviate the threat of flooding in the Pickering town area.

Approaching New Bridge, the NYMR's Permanent Way headquarters, established in 1983, is on the right, together with a locomotive stabling point, complete with inspection pit, which was constructed in 2006.

At New Bridge the line crosses the road from Pickering to Newton-on-Rawcliffe and Stape. The level crossing, together with all the signalling in the Pickering area, is controlled from the signal box, which dates from 1876. It once controlled a short spur into the adjacent quarry, but was closed when rail traffic ceased in 1966. BR removed the lever frame in 1969 but, although all the other disused signal boxes in the Pickering area were demolished, that at New Bridge survived. The NYMR subsequently set about refurbishing and re-equipping it, and it was recommissioned in 1986.

BR 2-6-4T No 80135 is photographed from the 13.20 Pickering-Grosmont train at Kingthorpe on 29 December 2000. *JH*

LNER 'B1' 4-6-0 No 61276 rounds Kingthorpe curves with the 4.08pm Malton-Whitby train in the summer of 1964. In the second picture, another 'B1', preserved No 61264, then in early BR green livery, is captured at the same location with a similar six-coach train. *David Sutcliffe/JH*

The first of these two views, looking southwards at New Bridge, was taken on 29 May 1965, two months after closure, and shows where the single line once again became double. The 'present' picture, taken on 12 September 2014, reveals that the NYMR running line has been slewed onto the previously lifted up formation, and the running line in the 1965 view is now a headshunt for the PW yard. *Frank Dean/JH*

LNER 'K4' 2-6-0 No 3442 *The Great Marquess* approaches New Bridge with the returning BBC filming special from Whitby to Leeds on 13 April 1964. On 29 October 2014 LMS 'Black Five' 4-6-0

No 45428 *Eric Treacy* passes the same spot with a through train from Whitby to Pickering. The pair of cottages on the left was built by the North Eastern Railway. *David Mitchell/JH*

The New Bridge signalman collects the single-line token from the crew of an unidentified LNER 'B1' 4-6-0 on an overcast summer's day in 1964. In the present-day scene the signaller prepares to do the same with the crew of another 'B1', No 61034 *Chiru*, on 18 September 2014. The spur into New Bridge quarry is evident on the left of the 'past' picture, and its route is marked by the garden hut in the 'present' equivalent. While the LNER warning sign on the right has gone, the concrete post still lies in the cess. *Frank Dean/JH*

In the early days of the NYMR, through trains over the whole length of the line were very rare and only ran on special occasions. This is one such occasion, when NCB 0-6-2T No 5 worked a two-coach train into Pickering carrying a deputation from the North Riding County Council on a fact-finding mission on 23 July 1971.

In March 1973, at the same location, are RSH 0-6-0T No 31 and Hudswell Clarke 0-6-0T No 20

Jennifer, while being unloaded on the other side of New Bridge level crossing is BR Standard 2-6-4T No 80135, just arrived from Barry scrapyard. In the 1971 picture the turnout into New Bridge quarry can just be made out in the grass on the left, and No 5 is using the down siding. In the lower picture a start has been made on relaying the former down line, but the up line – the one in use today – has yet to be relaid. *Both JH*

Celebrating 40 years of History
North Yorkshire Moors Railway
1973 - 2013

Pickering is an ancient market town and civil parish in the Ryedale district of North Yorkshire, on the border of the North York Moors National Park. Historically part of the North Riding of Yorkshire, it sits at the foot of the moors, overlooking the Vale of Pickering to the south. According to legend the town was founded by King Peredurus around 270BC; however, the town as it exists today is of medieval origin. The legend states that the town was named by King Peredurus; he lost his ring and accused a young maiden of stealing it, but later that day the ring was found in a pike caught that day in the River Costa for his dinner. The king was so happy to find his ring that he married the young maiden, and the name 'Pike-ring' got changed over the years to Pickering.

Pickering is not only the headquarters of the NYMR but its other attractions include the Parish Church, with its medieval wall paintings, Pickering Castle, and Beck Isle Museum, which have all made the town popular with visitors. It has a population of nearly 7,000, enjoys a street market on Mondays, and, since 1201, has stood at the major crossroads of the York-Whitby and Thirsk-Scarborough routes.

The railway was well placed to serve the town as it passed right through the centre, the station being a few yards from the Market Place. The early preservationists were eager to restore services to Pickering, but the initial efforts were thwarted by the then Pickering Urban District Council's intentions to demolish and redevelop the station. When services were extended beyond Goathland, they were diesel-operated to a temporary platform at High Mill, about half a mile north of the station, which had no run-round facility. Fortunately, the plans for the station were withdrawn following a public enquiry, and although the reopening Royal Train had special dispensation to use the station on 1 May 1973, it was to be 24 May 1975 before regular services would once again use Pickering station.

Since then, the station has been totally transformed and enhanced, as befits the headquarters of the NYMR. Dating from 1847, it was another example of a G.T. Andrews station, and was similar to those at Malton, Rillington Junction and Whitby by incorporating an overall roof. As well as the station, a goods shed, gas works, engine shed and various signal boxes, houses and cottages were also constructed in the Pickering area, several of which survive to this day.

Over the years no major alterations were made to the station until 1952, when BR removed the overall roof, but gradually, after closure, deterioration set in. However, once the difficulties over the future of the station had been overcome and trains started using it, the process of gradual improvement and enhancement commenced. A locomotive run-round facility was installed at the south end, sidings were laid, a water tank and two water columns erected, and colour light signalling introduced, controlled from New Bridge.

Between 1979 and 1983 a carriage and wagon shed was erected just north of the station, to accommodate, repair and maintain the railway's ever-growing collection of carriages and wagons. The facility has been slowly enlarged and improved over the subsequent years. In 2008 a new carriage restoration shed was built for the LNER Coach Association and named the Atkins Building, after the benefactor who gave the legacy to enable it to be built; it is used for all timber rolling stock conservation.

However, it was the late 1990s before any wholesale changes to the station itself took place. In 1992/93 a building from Whitby station was re-erected on Platform 1 to provide accommodation for retail and catering stores and offices, and in 1994 the turntable pit was excavated and a 60-foot turntable from York was installed. In 1996 the NER footbridge from Walkergate on Tyneside was erected to connect Platforms 1 and 2 and the footpath to the railway's car park beyond the carriage shed, and in 1999 another wooden building, this time from Gilling, was reconstructed north of the Whitby building on Platform 1 to provide accommodation for platform staff. In 1999/2000 Platform 1 was extended northwards to provide accommodation for eight-coach trains, and major refurbishment works took place on the main station buildings. The booking

office was restored to its former use and the parcels office became the NYMR's Customer Services office. The former Station Master's office, general room and gentlemen's 1st class waiting room became the railway's tea room, and the porters' room, ladies' waiting room and lavatory were transformed into a shop. The current toilets share the space originally occupied by the larger gentlemen's toilet and are fitted out to modern standards, and with period tiling. The original platform surface consists of stone slabs up to 12 feet wide, between 12 and 15 feet long, and weighing around 3 to 4 tons. The NER looked at heightening the platforms in 1870, but concluded that 'the platforms at Pickering station could not be conveniently raised. Ordered: movable steps be provided for the use of passengers there', a solution that is still in use today!

It was the period between 2009 and 2014 that saw the most significant changes, however. With generous funding from a variety of sources, but particularly the Heritage Lottery Fund, Yorkshire Forward and Yorventure, the Train of Thought Project was instigated. This initially provided a two-storey learning centre behind the wall on Platform 2, which comprises lecture/exhibition rooms and, importantly, the NYMR archive. Upon opening in 2010, it was named the Reussner Learning Centre, after the railway's late archivist, Graham Reussner. To the north of the centre, the original pump house was refurbished to provide the Yorventure visitor centre. The most impressive aspect and crowning glory of the project was the rebuilding of the overall roof in 2010/11. A virtually exact copy of the original was designed and constructed using similar techniques to the original, including the use of riveted joints. The so-called Euston Truss design also incorporates internal boarding to provide diagonal bracing, and the roof is covered by 8,700 slates from Penrhyn quarry at Bethesda in North Wales, many of them individually sponsored.

Above left: The banner says it all! NCB 0-6-2T No 29 pilots LNER 'K1' 2-6-0 No 62005 into Pickering station, beneath the superb new overall roof, on 1 May 2013. *JH*

Right: The unusual 'running-in sign' at Pickering. *JH*

This is High Mill level crossing, looking north, in October 1964. The two running lines are on the extreme right, the line in the centre being the down siding. The signal box was demolished in 1970 and there is now just one running line, although the siding full of coaches in the 'present' picture is the old down line. The trees on the left and the houses on the right are common to both views. *Frank Dean/ JH*

LNER 'B1' 4-6-0 No 61319 brings the daily Whitby-York goods into Pickering on a dreary day in November 1964. The train has just passed No 15 signal, which controlled entry to the station and was situated on the down side to allow better sighting from up trains; the High Mill signaller must have returned it quickly to danger following passage of the train! The siding on the extreme left led to the turntable.

It may be hard to believe, but the second picture was taken from the same viewpoint, on 18 September 2014, and depicts fellow 'B1' No 61264, temporarily masquerading as No 61034 *Chiru*, entering the station with a train from Whitby. The up platform has been extended northwards, carriage sheds now occupy the siding area on the left, and trees hide the gable of High Mill itself. *Frank Dean/JH*

At the north end of the down platform stood a water column and water tower, pictured here on a dismal day in November 1964, and demolished by 1966.

The trees on the right horizon are also recognisable in the second picture, which shows that the water column and tower have disappeared and in their place the NYMR's carriage shed is in the throes of construction in March 1979.

The same view on 10 November 2013 shows the completed carriage shed, with the single-road paint shop subsequently added on the left of the picture. In the distance is the Atkins Building carriage restoration shed and, hidden beyond the coaches, the turntable. In the foreground is the bridge over the Pickering Beck. *Frank Dean/JH (2)*

Robert Stephenson & Hawthorn 0-4-0ST No 15 *Eustace Forth* shunts a BR 20T brake van at Pickering station on 27 August 1973 during a special event, while in the second picture the buildings in the background, in Park Street, and the spire of the parish church identify it as the same location as BR

4-6-0 No 75029 *The Green Knight* takes water on 15 December 2013. In the intervening period double track and sidings have been laid, the up platform extended, a water column erected, and colour light signals installed. *Chris Gammell/JH*

This rather desolate view of Pickering station, looking south, dates from December 1970. Although the station nameboard still stands, weeds are gradually taking over. Bridge Street signal box can be glimpsed beyond the station.

In the 'present' view, taken on 18 September 2014, the transformation is complete! Prominent are the new overall roof and the footbridge. Note the difference in height between the original platform and the extension, and the moveable steps. *P. Walton/JH*

Looking at this view in the opposite direction at around the same time, few can have visualised how Pickering station would eventually evolve. High Mill, proclaiming its last user, W. Lumley & Son, is prominent in the background, and one of the towers of the castle can be seen on the right.

More than 40 years later, on 10 November 2013, the view is totally different. Both platforms have been extended northwards, the C&W paint shop is on the left and new platform buildings are on the right. The bridge over the Pickering Beck has also been rebuilt. Trees now hide High Mill and the castle. *NYMR archive/JH*

The view from the down platform in December 1970 contrasts markedly with the similar view on 19 November 2013. New buildings comprise the Station Foremen's hut, on the left, recovered from Gilling, while the larger building came from Whitby Town and now houses retail and catering stores and offices. Despite the tree growth, the houses in the background are still recognisable. *P. Walton/JH*

The station looks well used and in good condition in the first view, on the penultimate day of passenger operation, 5 March 1965.

Following closure, the station was badly neglected pending a decision on its future, and was devoid of fittings and becoming weed infested when the second picture was taken in December 1970.

What a contrast in the third view! Restoration of a G.T. Andrews-style overall roof took place in 2010/11 and what a difference it makes, as this view taken on 10 November 2013 illustrates. The large stone slabs forming the original platform surface can be seen. *Frank Dean/P. Walton/JH*

LNER 'K4' 2-6-0 No 3442 *The Great Marquess* attracts the attention of photographers as it pauses in the station with the BBC filming special returning from Whitby to Leeds on 13 April 1964.

In almost the same place LMS 'Black Five, 4-6-0 No 45428 *Eric Treacy* prepares to run round its train on 1 November 2014. Although the track layout has been simplified and the loading dock removed, the NYMR installed a siding to accommodate stores vans and recreate the former appearance. *David Mitchell/JH*

Viewed from the loading bank, LNER 'B1' 4-6-0 No 61319 awaits the signal with a Whitby-York passenger train in July 1964. The 'present' picture shows fellow 'B1' No 61034 *Chiru* (in reality No 61264) about to run round its train on 18

September 2014. At the end of the down platform the signal box recovered from Marishes Road, extensively rebuilt, has been repositioned to provide a demonstration signal box. *Frank Dean/JH*

These two views were taken from the end of the down platform looking towards the town centre and Bridge Street level crossing on 6 March 1965 and 17 December 2013. Prominent in both pictures is the bank at the bottom of the Market Place, but the other buildings are unchanged too. *David Sutcliffe/JH*

PICKERING, YORKSHIRE

From a Water Colour by JACK MERRIOTT, R.I.

This railway carriage print of Pickering Market Place was taken from a water colour painting by Jack Merriott RI, and it is accompanied by the same view today. Whilst the buildings in the middle of the painting have been demolished, the others are instantly recognisable. *JH*

In the view of the station from Bridge Street, taken in October 1964, there is a wealth of track and signalling detail and a clear view of the loading dock. In the present-day equivalent, taken on 17 December 2013, the track has been simplified and an NER bogie stores van now occupies the site of the loading dock, but on an isolated piece of track. The surrounding buildings remain the same – even the telegraph pole has survived! *Frank Dean/JH*

Bridge Street signal box, seen here in March 1965, probably dated from 1876 and controlled not only the busy level crossing but also train movements at the south end of the station and into and out of the goods yard. The cantilevered window on the north gable allowed the signalman to observe road traffic in Bridge Street.

The box was closed in 1965 and had been demolished by 1970. The site is now a pleasant paved area and, while the road junction has been enlarged, the modern road signs still direct traffic to Newton-on-Rawcliffe and Stape! *Frank Dean/JH*

Crossing Bridge Street and entering the station is LNER 'K4' 2-6-0 No 3442 *The Great Marquess* with the BBC filming special on 13 April 1964. Though the crossing has gone and the station altered, the buildings on the left and in the right distance are the same. *David Mitchell/JH*

Immediately south of Bridge Street the railway crossed the Pickering Beck; the two running lines are nearest the camera in this March 1965 view, while furthest away are the sidings coming out of the goods yard, controlled by an LNER ground signal. Note the period cars and bus outside the station.

The equivalent view on 17 December 2013 shows that the road bridge has used the old railway bridge abutments, though on a slightly different alignment. *Frank Dean/JH*

LNER 'K4' 2-6-0 No 3442 *The Great Marquess* is seen once again, slowing for the Pickering stop with the BBC filming special from Leeds to Whitby on 13 April 1964. It is passing LNER 'B1' 4-6-0 No 61021 *Reitbok* shunting the York-Whitby goods in the goods yard. Above the 'B1' stands the York & North Midland Railway gas retort house.

The present-day view from the same vantage point on 24 November 2014 is looking down what is now known as The Ropery, but the retort house still stands. *David Mitchell/JH*

The gas retort house is seen here on 1 July 1966. As well as the fine station building, the Y&NMR also provided other characteristic Andrews buildings, including a stone-built goods shed, with wooden extension, and a gas works – one of the earliest surviving railway gas works buildings – which occupied the area now known as 'The Ropery'. While the goods shed was demolished to make way for the new road, the gas works retort and purifier house still stands today, adjacent to the new road. It ceased to produce gas when Pickering got its own gas and water company, and the North Eastern Railway converted it into a corn warehouse. By the 1960s it was occupied by a tyre retailer and was subsequently restored for use as a cafe, later becoming a ladies' hairdresser. When the adjacent doctor's surgery was being built, the base of the gas holder was discovered and excavated, still smelling of coal gas. It was filled in, sealed off and built over. The 'present' view was taken on 17 December 2013. *Frank Dean/JH*

Left: Hudswell Clarke 0-4-0ST *Mirvale* was the first steam locomotive to arrive on the infant NYMR. Here it begins its epic journey from Bridge Street to Grosmont on 2 February 1969.

Below: Looking at the same location on 17 December 2013, the buildings are still recognisable, though Bridge Street signal box has gone. *John Boyes/JH*

Below and below right: Borrows 0-4-0WT No 3 stands on its low-loader in the Eastgate car park in March 1969, prior to unloading at the old goods yard. In the same scene today The Royal Oak is on the left and a new generation of cars occupies the car park. *John Boyes/JH*

Andrew Barclay 0-6-0ST *Salmon* was the second steam locomotive to arrive, and is seen here being unloaded in the old goods yard. Together with No 3, it was steamed through to Grosmont on 30 March 1969.

The same vantage point on 17 December 2013 reveals that the new road, The Ropery, now runs through the old goods yard and, while the goods shed has gone, the bank in the background remains. *John Boyes/JH*

The 'past' view, taken in March 1965, shows the small brick-built single-road engine shed, large enough for a single locomotive, built by the York & North Midland Railway. The shed was extended by the NER in 1867, retaining the same style, and a standard Y&NMR house was built adjacent to it. In the distance can be seen Mill Lane signal box, and on the right the wall of the coal drops.

Both buildings are still standing today, though incorporated into a joinery works, as shown in the second picture taken on 2 September 2014. This building is not only a rare (if not unique) surviving example of a G. T. Andrews engine shed, but it is one of very few rural, single-track engine sheds still standing. The coal drops wall also survives, as does the bridge over the Pickering Beck. *Frank Dean/JH*

Another milestone day was 1 July 1966, when the last remaining goods traffic ceased. Following closure of the line from Grosmont, the section from Rillington Junction to the quarry at New Bridge remained open for freight. The 'past' view was taken from the cab of No D2066 leaving Pickering with the final train; to the right of the wagons can be seen the single-road locomotive shed.

To obtain the 'present' equivalent on 17 December 2013 entailed standing on top of a stepladder on a playing field! The building behind the tall tree in the 'past' picture can be clearly seen in the modern view, and the roof of the engine shed can just be discerned. *Frank Dean/JH*

A Metro-Cammell DMU passes Mill Lane level crossing forming a Whitby-Malton working in January 1965. The signal is off for the Rillington Junction line; the other arm used to control the Forge Valley line towards Scarborough, but at the time of this picture the final stretch of line to Thornton-le-Dale had been lifted. The track on the left was a siding that served the coal drops, which can be seen straight ahead in the distance. Also in the distance can be glimpsed Hungate level crossing. The junction of the line westward to Kirkbymoorside and Helmsley was behind the camera.

In the 'present' picture, taken on 15 December 2013, the only recognisable features are the G.T. Andrews crossing-keeper's cottage on the right and Mill Lane itself. *Frank Dean/JH*

In this view of Mill Lane in January 1965, the remains of the branch to Kirkbymoorside and Helmsley are on the left. Looking from the same vantage point on 15 December 2013, there is absolutely no trace of the railway. *Frank Dean/JH*

This is the junction between the Rillington and Forge Valley lines just south of Mill Lane in January 1965. Track-lifting had, by this time, reached the junction, but eerily the signal controlling the exit from the branch still stands sentinel.

Although all evidence of the former railway lines has disappeared under fields and housing, the two electricity supply poles and the slate-roofed former railway cottages in the distance appear in both pictures. *Frank Dean/JH*

Pickering to Malton

The 6¾-mile double track line from Pickering to Rillington Junction was built by the York & North Midland Railway and opened at the same time as the company's York-Malton-Scarborough line on 7 July 1845, thus linking the Whitby & Pickering Railway to the wider network. It ran across the flat land of the Vale of Pickering, so there were no substantial works involved in its construction, other than the crossing of the River Derwent near Low Marishes, a station at Marishes Road, and a number of level crossings.

Rillington Junction was 4½ miles east of Malton and possessed an overall station roof and a bay platform on the down side connected only to the Whitby line. The station was an early casualty when it closed on 20 September 1930, together with all the other intermediate stations between York and Scarborough (except Malton and Seamer). Despite early closure, the overall roof did not eventually go until 1955.

On 1 July 1865 the North Eastern Railway had opened a north-to-east curve at Rillington in an effort to encourage traffic between Whitby and Scarborough via Pickering, long before the coastal route and Forge

Valley lines opened. It was not a success and closed on 1 March 1874, the track being lifted in 1880. A curved fence line and a brick cabin at High Scampston are reminders of the course of this long-closed line.

Following closure of the through route on 6 March 1965, one of the lines remained in use for the goods traffic to and from Pickering New Bridge until that too ceased, the last train running on 1 July 1966. Subsequently the track was lifted, the final scrap train being hauled by Class 40 diesel No D399 on 2 November 1969.

Because of the flat nature of the land over which the railway ran, much of the trackbed has reverted to agricultural use, although here and there hedge lines, fences and farm tracks mark the course of the railway. What have survived, however, are the lineside houses and cottages, still in residential use – they were obviously built to last!

Over recent years there have been suggestions that one day the railway might return between Rillington and Pickering, and although the trackbed has been built on in one or two places, perhaps one should never say never!

Marishes Road station, looking north, in January 1965. *David Sutcliffe*

Black Bull level crossing is seen here in January 1965, with a typical G. T. Andrews crossing-keeper's cottage on the left. This was a busy crossing, as the road is the main A169 between Malton, Pickering and Whitby. On 17 December 2013 there is no evidence that there was ever a railway or level crossing here; only the cottage remains. *Frank Dean/JH*

These views towards Pickering along the A169 were taken on the same day as the previous two pictures, with the level crossing in the distance. In the 'present' picture, the crossing has long gone and there is more road traffic, but the Black Bull Inn has changed little. *Frank Dean/JH*

At Upper Carr, just south of Black Bull crossing – which is visible in the background – there was a more elaborate building, which was, from 1845 to 1858, Black Bull or Kirby station building. The 'past' view was taken after complete closure, as the rails are rusty and the signal arms have gone. An interesting survivor, however, is the rather primitive signal, a rotating board (another is pictured at Low Marishes on page 117). It was turned to face the railway when the crossing was open to the road and to the road when a train was coming. As well as Upper Carr, Low Marishes and Farwath, many other level crossings kept them right through to closure.

Although altered slightly, the old station building remains in use as a private residence, as the present-day view, taken on 17 December 2013, shows. *Frank Dean/JH*

A Metro-Cammell DMU forming a Whitby-Malton service arrives at Marishes Road station in January 1965. Remarkably, as the second picture taken on 17 December 2013 illustrates, the station is still intact, complete with station house, platforms and down-side waiting shelter – waiting, perchance, for the trains to return? The signal box was dismantled by the NYMR in 1969 and moved to Goathland; later, heavily rebuilt, it was relocated at Pickering in 2013. *Frank Dean/JH*

The same train departs towards Rillington Junction. There was a siding on the up side, accessed from a turnout hidden by the DMU. Beyond the trees on the right-hand horizon was Low Marishes. The 'present' picture was taken from the identical vantage point. *Frank Dean/JH*

Low Marishes crossing-keeper's cottage is seen on 15 May 1965; note the rotating red signal board (see also page 114). In the corresponding view, dated 17 December 2013, the cottage, seemingly unaltered externally save for a coat of render, appears in excellent condition. *Frank Dean/JH*

This was the view looking north from Low Marishes level crossing, also on 15 May 1965. At this time the only traffic was the goods train to and from Pickering New Bridge, which used the old down line in both directions. In the present-day view from 17 December 2013, a farm track now follows the old railway formation. *Frank Dean/JH*

Photographed from the top of the Rillington Junction down starting signal on 9 March 1968, we see the by now totally disused line to Pickering; the long abandoned north-to-east spur is marked by the line of bushes at the top of the ploughed field on the right.

On 19 December 2013, looking from the top of a stepladder in the absence of the signal, the hedge line marks the former railway alignment. *Frank Dean/ JH*

This is the view from the brake van of the final goods train from Pickering New Bridge on 1 July 1966 as it approaches the junction with the main Scarborough-York line at Rillington Junction. In the present-day equivalent the curving fence line on the left marks the course of the former branch, while the farmhouse in the middle distance is just visible through the trees on 19 December 2013. *Frank Dean/JH*

Rillington Junction station was photographed, 35 years after closure, on 6 March 1965, the day of the Whitby closures, with melted snow on the down platform. In the 'present' picture, taken on 19 December 2013, the main station building remains, modernised for its current use as a private residence, and the level crossing has been automated. *Frank Dean/JH*

In December 1964 an Class 03 0-6-0 diesel shunter trundles past Rillington signal box on its way to Malton. In the present-day picture, taken on 19 December 2013, a Class 185 DMU hurries towards Scarborough. The signal box dated from 1959, having replaced an NER box next to the actual junction. It lasted until 31 October 1993, when the level crossing was converted to half barriers and signalling control transferred to Malton East signal box. Although the station building on the down side, the platforms and the signal box have gone, the NER 1890s-built cottages on the left and the main station building survive. *Frank Dean/JH*

Malton

Malton is a market town of around 13,000 people, located to the north of the River Derwent, which forms the historic boundary between the North and East Ridings of Yorkshire. Facing Malton, on the other side of the Derwent, is Norton. Malton is the local area's commercial and retail centre.

The railway came to Malton with the opening of the York & North Midland Railway's line from York to Scarborough on 7 July 1845. The station was designed by G. T. Andrews, incorporating one of his distinctive overall roofs, beneath which ran two tracks. Subsequently one of these was removed so that the down platform could be widened, which gave rise to a possibly unique feature of Malton station – a drawbridge! It was unusual in that it ran on wheels at right angles across the track to give access for passengers to the up island platform in the absence of a footbridge. Interlocked with the signalling, it could be retracted beneath the platform whenever a train needed to enter the down platform. At the east end of the station there were sidings and a bay platform primarily for Whitby trains; this was covered by a glazed roof designed by NER architect William Bell, and erected in 1883. Thirty years earlier, in 1853, a two-road locomotive shed had been built on the south side of the line at the west end of the station; it was extended in 1867. There were goods yards at both ends of the station, on the north side.

'Railway Mania' was at its height and further lines were added when the York, Newcastle & Berwick Railway opened its Thirsk and Malton line on 19 May 1853. Three months later, the Malton & Driffield Railway (M&DR) opened its line from Driffield. The latter joined the York-Scarborough line just east of Malton station, but the Thirsk line, instead of running directly into Malton station, crossed the main line and met the M&DR at Scarborough Road Junction in Norton; trains from the Thirsk direction then had to reverse direction to gain access to Malton station..

In the wake of the closures of the Driffield line on 18 October 1958, the remaining part of the Thirsk line on 19 October 1964, and the Whitby line on 6 March 1965, the first half of 1966 saw track and signalling simplified and modernised in the Malton area. The York-bound island platform was abandoned, together with the famous drawbridge, and surplus track at the west end, the engine shed and the Whitby bay were removed. The semaphore signals were replaced by colour lights controlled by Malton East signal box, and the remaining two signal boxes were closed. All stopping passenger trains used the former down platform, which therefore became bi-directional, though the up line was retained for non-stop trains.

A Metro-Cammell DMU waits to leave the down platform with a train for Whitby in April 1964. On the left is Malton signal box and the engine shed. *John Spencer Gilks*

Respectably clean BR Standard 2-6-0 No 77012 stands in the bay platform at Malton with the 4.00pm train to Whitby in the winter of 1963. This was the final passenger turn covered by Malton shed, which closed on 15 April that year.

Following rationalisation in 1966 the bay platform tracks were removed, but the awning was not demolished until 1989, when parts were reused to extend the canopy on the remaining platform following demolition of the overall roof. On 19 December 2013 a supermarket occupies the site of the bay platform and goods yard, though the platform edge remains. *Frank Dean/JH*

The view eastwards from beneath the station roof on 16 June 1965 shows the bay platform on the left and the island platform on the right. Malton East signal box can just be discerned above the wall in the middle distance.

In the same view some time in 1966 the sidings in the bay platform have been removed, and two Metro-Cammell DMUs are leaving for Scarborough.

Looking from the same vantage point on 19 December 2013, it can be seen how much has changed. *Frank Dean/John Spencer Gilks/JH*

A Class 150 single-car unit, No 150254, pauses at Malton with a York-Scarborough working in October 1988. Although by that time the island platform had been removed and up and down trains were using the former down platform, the overall roof still stood, eventually succumbing in 1989.

In the comparative view, taken on 24 November 2014, unit No 185103 calls as the 11.50 Scarborough-Liverpool Lime Street service. The two sidings nearest the camera remain, and the third track is the up line for non-stop trains. *John Spencer Gilks/JH*

This is the view of the goods yard, west of the station, in the 1970s. In its heyday Malton handled oil, livestock and coal (the line to the coal drops is in the middle of the first picture). In the distance can be seen the water tank, pump house and stables, while the milepost records 21 miles from York. Goods facilities were withdrawn on 23 September 1984 after the yard had already been reduced to public delivery siding status; the track was lifted in 1991.

In the 'present' view, taken on 19 December 2013, the site has been redeveloped for housing and the station car park. The church spire on the left and the station buildings on the right are common to both pictures. *John Spencer Gilks/JH*

On 14 May 1964 LNER 'B1' 4-6-0 No 61018 *Gnu* shunts the 6.45am York-Whitby goods at the west end of the station. There is an interesting display of signals, controlled by Malton signal box, out of sight to the left, and Malton West signal box in the distance. These boxes closed in 1966 when the layout was altered and colour light signalling replaced the semaphores, controlled from Malton East signal box. On the left is the two-road engine shed.

In the present picture colour light signals have replaced the semaphores, as a Class 185 DMU approaches forming the 07.15 Liverpool Lime Street-Scarborough service on 24 November 2014. Interestingly, the main-to-main crossover remains in the same place! *John Boyes/JH*